"Dr. Dennis Merritt Jones has created a classic that belongs right next to the other metaphysical dictionaries. This will become a reliable friend in deepening one's understanding of the spiritual truths within Science of Mind."

REV. CHRISTIAN SORENSEN, D.D., Seaside Center for Spiritual Living, CA

"This outstanding book is a must for everyone in New Thought . . . In fact, I think this is one of the best books of its kind in the history of New Thought. Spread the word. Use it in every class. It is too good to miss!"

DR. JAY SCOTT NEALE, Center for Spiritual Living, Fremont CA

". . . An invaluable tool of information and clarity for all of our guests, followers, and students. I am excited about the revised content reflecting the shifting consciousness and birth of an even bigger idea for New Thought."

REV. PATRICK CAMERON, Edmonton's Centre for Spiritual Living

"Dr. Jones' gift of clarity and simplicity is refreshing. *How to Speak Science of Mind* offers the reader an opportunity to thoroughly understand and clearly articulate the terms and principles of Science of Mind."

REV. CHRIS MICHAELS, Center for Spiritual Living, Kansas City MO

"...We always keep a generous supply of *How to Speak Science of Mind* on hand. We use it in our classes and for first time attendees who want to know more about the Science of Mind."

DR. MAUREEN HOYT, Center for Spiritual Living, Westlake Village CA

"A wonderful reflection of the truth of our philosophy which proves the point that while language changes, Truth does not. This is an excellent source of insight and clarity not only for students of Science of Mind, but indeed for the millions of individuals who are awakening to their spiritual magnificence."

DR. KENN GORDON, President, International Centers for Spiritual Living

"How to Speak Science of Mind is the quintessential tour-guide for the spiritual traveler. I take mine with me wherever I go. Don't leave home without it!"

REV. DAVID BRUNER, Center for Spiritual Living, San Jose CA

"*How To Speak Science of Mind* is a treasury of new thought wisdom ... an enriching and enlightening spiritual tool."

REV. MOIRA FOX, Redondo Beach Center for Spiritual Living

THE PURPOSE OF THIS BOOK

*The world is tired of mysteries, does not understand
symbols, and longs for Reality. What is Reality?
Where may It be found? How may It be used?
These are the questions we should like to have answered.*

—DR. ERNEST HOLMES
The Science of Mind Textbook

This book has been created to assist the person who is on
the pathway of Self-discovery in revealing the answer to
the above questions.

HOW TO SPEAK
SCIENCE OF MIND

By Dennis Merritt Jones, D.D.

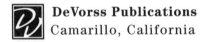
DeVorss Publications
Camarillo, California

Library of Congress Control Number: 2010931170
ISBN13: 978-0-87516-858-6
FOURTH PRINTING, 2023

DeVorss & Company, Publisher
P.O. Box 1389
Camarillo CA 93011-1389
www.devorss.com

Printed in the United States of America

WHAT IS SCIENCE OF MIND?

Science of Mind is a spiritual teaching and way of life based on the inspirations of Dr. Ernest Holmes and his book, *The Science of Mind*. Science of Mind exists to facilitate the reawakening of each individual's awareness of the higher Self, enabling all who desire to discover and know the ultimate Oneness of Universal Life to do so. While sometimes mistaken for Scientology or Christian Science because of name similarities, we are neither. The teachings offered in Science of Mind are not in opposition to any religious belief or philosophy. Rather, they seek to bring to light the thread of Truth that exists in all spiritual teachings.

Ernest Holmes (1887-1960) founded the original Religious Science organization that taught and supported the Science of Mind philosophy within the New Thought movement. Schooled in Christian Science, he moved to Los Angeles in 1912. Holmes published his first book, *Creative Mind* in 1919, and followed it up with *The Science of Mind* in 1926. Holmes had an immense influence on New Thought.

Science of Mind recognizes that all people are on a path to their own fulfillment and must be guided by their own inner voice. We offer practical and definite methods with which each individual can create positive life changes. Among the benefits of the teachings of Science of Mind is the understanding of affirmative prayer or spiritual mind healing. We refer to this as Spiritual Mind Treatment.

In summary, Science of Mind offers healing, spiritual understanding, and an opportunity to experience greater love, greater joy, and greater life expression. In the words of Dr. Ernest Holmes, "There is a power for good in the universe greater than you are, and you can use it!"

....

Divine Truth Never Needs To Be Sold, Just Told!

LISTED ON THE FOLLOWING PAGES are words that most often come up while discussing what we believe with those who may be of a different spiritual background.

The definitions of these words are offered as tools to better help explain Science of Mind and enhance one's ability to communicate with others. Communication is the key to all relationships. Our goal in discussing our beliefs with others is not to convert or "save" anyone, nor is it to try to prove one is "right" or the other, "wrong." Our goal is to inform and educate. The Infinite Intelligence within all people will know if the teachings of Science of Mind are right for a particular person.

....

ABSOLUTE

ABUNDANCE

AFFIRMATION

ATONEMENT

BEING

BLESSING

BIBLE

CAUSE AND EFFECT

CHRIST

CHRISTIAN

COLLECTIVE MIND

CONSCIOUSNESS

CULT

DEATH

DENIAL

DEMONSTRATION

DESTINY

DEVIL

DIAGNOSIS

DISEASE

DIVINE URGE

DOCTORS AND
  MEDICINE

DUALITY

EMBODY

ENERGY

ETERNAL

EVIL

FAITH

FEAR

GOD

GRACE

HEALING

HEAVEN

HELL

I AM

IMMORTALITY

INTUITION

JESUS

JUDGMENT

KARMA

LAW OF MIND

LOVE

MACROCOSM &
  MICROCOSM

MEDITATION

METAPHYSICS

MIND

MINDFULNESS

MONEY

NEW AGE

NEW THOUGHT

OMNIPOTENCE

OMNIPRESENCE

OMNISCIENCE

PRACTITIONER

PRAYER

PRINCIPLE

PUNISHMENT

REALITY

REALIZATION

REINCARNATION

RELATIVE

RELIGION

RELIGIOUS SCIENCE

RESURRECTION

RIGHT ACTION

SAVIOR

SCIENCE OF MIND

SIN

SOUL

SPIRIT

SPIRITUALITY

THOUGHT

TREATMENT

TRUTH

UNIVERSE

VISIONING

WORD

DECLARATIONS AND
  PRINCIPLES

Is Absolute another word for God?

Yes, Absolute is another word for God. The truth is, God is all there is. As absolute being, God is infinite, perfect, unlimited, unconditioned, self-existent, and all self-sufficient. It could be said that in the beginning there was only God...and there still is only God.

[See Reality]

Is there a difference between Abundance and Prosperity?

We live in a prolific and abundant universe. We need only to look to the skies or nature to see a demonstration of abundance as a universal principle. The universe is expanding at the speed of light and there are hundreds of millions of stars and galaxies. The message God is sending us is, there is more than enough.

Abundance is the principle of "more than enough" and prosperity is our demonstration of that principle in action. In *The Science of Mind*, Ernest Holmes states, "Prosperity is the out-picturing of substance in our affairs...we must receive, utilize and extend the gift." There is no shortage of anything good in the universe but there appears to be a lack of understanding of how to access that good and keep it flowing.

We can be prosperous in many different ways, demonstrating an abundance of physical health, healthy relationships, money, time, and so on. Developing a consciousness of abundance will open the floodgates of our good. This consciousness is based in an awareness of our oneness with God; the Source and Supply of it all.

[See Money and Energy]

Do we use affirmations?
What purpose do they serve?

....

In *The Science of Mind*, Ernest Holmes states, "To affirm anything is to state that it is so, and to maintain this as being true in the face of all evidence to the contrary." In the practice of Spiritual Mind Treatment, also known as Affirmative Prayer, affirmations are used to build a consciousness of receptivity and expectation of good.

When we use positive affirmations such as, "The perfect health and vitality of God flow through my entire being," we are stating a fact we know is true, even if appearances may not support that statement. We know it is the truth because we know we are one with God. Stating affirmations is a good practice; however, it is important that we also embody the feeling behind the words we use.

[See Treatment and Embody]

Do we practice atonement in Science of Mind?

． ． ． ． ． ． ． ． ． ． ． ． ． ． ． ． ．

In traditional theology atonement is the doctrine concerning the reconciliation of God and humankind. We do not believe that God could be or would be separate from us because we are always one with God. However, there may be times we may need to reconcile ourselves with God because we have wrongly believed that we are separate from God. Metaphysically, when we practice atonement we are affirming our "at-one-ment" with God. Atonement happens when we heal any sense of apartness from God—when we return to our original awareness of our unity with the Divine Whole.

Is Being used as a noun or a verb?

In *The Science of Mind*, Ernest Holmes states, "When capitalized, Being refers to the Divine Being, God. There is but one Source of being—God—and we are connected with It at all times."

The practice for us is to take our Divine Being into our daily doing. By incorporating the awareness of our unity with God into the activities of our daily life, Being/being is both a noun and a verb.

What does it mean to bless?

....

In Science of Mind, to bless anyone or anything is to confer and confirm our awareness of God's presence in that which we bless.

It is a beneficial practice to bless our food because it reminds us of the Source whence it comes and our bodies receive the benefit of that blessing. To bless our relationships means to remember that every person is a sacred Being and can be treated as such. To bless our work is to remember God's presence at the center of every transaction. To bless our world is to confirm our belief that Infinite Presence is working in and through all people and all events for the highest and best for all concerned.

Remembering to bless our lives and the lives of others every day will transform us, them, and our world.

Do we use it? Do we take it literally?

Ernest Holmes, the author of *The Science of Mind*, was greatly influenced by the Bible and it is a cornerstone of his teachings. However, he made it clear that it is important to understand the metaphysical meaning of the Bible and that not all of it can be taken literally.

The Bible was written 2,000 to 3,000 years ago by the Semitic people, for the Semitic people. The Bible is a valuable and valid source of Truth when read and understood according to the authors' consciousness and heritage. Truth is Truth, and the Bible must be read with an open mind, looking for the higher meaning in the stories, metaphors, and parables. To fully understand the Bible, one must understand idioms and the psychology used by the men who wrote the book. Yes, God did write the Bible, through the consciousness of human beings; therefore, we must understand humankind to understand the book.

What is the difference between Cause and Effect?

....

Cause is always that which produces an effect. Metaphysically, we are always becoming cause to our own effect through our thinking and deepest beliefs [see Consciousness]. Our conscious mind is that point where cause begins. The effect or result is reflected in our physical bodies and the body of our affairs. When we become aware of this process, we find that as we change the cause (our thinking), the effect (our lives) changes automatically. As practitioners of Science of Mind, we deal in cause rather than effect.

[See Thought]

Was Jesus the Christ?

. . . .

It's important to understand that Christ was not Jesus' last name; it is a title which acknowledges the fact that he fully understood and demonstrated his divine nature and his oneness with God.

The word "Christ" comes from the Greek word *Christos*, which means "anointed" or "enlightened one." In *The Science of Mind*, Ernest Holmes states, "Christ is a universal idea, and each one 'puts on the Christ' to the degree that he surrenders a limited sense of life to the Divine Realization of wholeness and unity with Good, Spirit, God."

Do we consider ourselves Christians?

....

A "Christian" by definition is one who:

1. Believes in Jesus Christ as one's Lord and Savior; and,
2. Follows his teachings.

In the traditional sense, we do not consider ourselves Christian because we do not claim the man Jesus as our "Lord and Savior" [see Savior]. However, we do believe in his teachings upon which the Science of Mind textbook is largely based. We believe that the teacher Jesus came to show us each the way of the Christ. [see Christ]

Therefore, it is up to all individuals to analyze their own life to decide if they are "Christian" or not. The message of the Christ is unconditional love, non-judgment, forgiveness, brotherhood, peace and oneness with God. Perhaps true Christianity is more of a lifestyle than it is any one particular religion.

What is Collective Mind and how does it affect the individual?

When *The Science of Mind* was written by Ernest Holmes, he referred to collective mind as race-mind because it held the conscious and unconscious thoughts, energy, and ideas of the entire human race. Also referred to as the collective unconscious or social belief system, collective mind is a thought force that permeates the entire planet.

What Holmes referred to as race-suggestion had nothing to do with ethnicity or specific cultures; it is the collective human belief system operating through the mentality of any individual in the human race who is open and receptive to it. If we are not aware, it is quite easy to slip into the vibration and influence of nonproductive thought and become subject to how it operates through collective mind.

The collective mind can be a prolific source of negative energy. We can rise above the vibration of collective negative thought by consciously focusing our daily awareness upon a higher reality. The negative aspects of collective mind cannot operate through those who are fully aware of God's presence in and around them.

What and where is consciousness?

. . . .

Our consciousness is our mental awareness. It is both the conscious and the subconscious mind and all they contain. In essence, our consciousness is the sum total of everything we have ever believed and accepted to be the truth about ourselves from the moment we were born until this moment in time.

Our consciousness is how we make individual use of Universal Mind. Our consciousness forms a belief system into which Life pours Itself [see Mind]. We can change our consciousness through Spiritual Mind Treatment [see Prayer]. The ultimate consciousness we want to develop would embrace an awareness that "God Is All There Is."

Are we a cult?

According to the dictionary, a cult is a group which studies a system of religious worship in admiration of, or devotion to, a person or thing.

In the teachings of Science of Mind we worship no one nor any thing. To do so would be idolatry. We believe we need no one to intercede between ourselves and God. Unlike some teachings that have begun to teach the worship of the messenger instead of teaching the message, Science of Mind is the furthest thing from being a cult. Our teaching is universal, "in the open," and places no one above or below ourselves. We believe God is available to one and all equally.

Do we believe in death?

The divine principle of Life is an eternally unfolding, upward-spiraling movement. The spirit of God is the spirit of life, and it is both birthless and deathless. The principle of life cannot know death. Life itself cannot be destroyed— only the form it occupies can be altered.

In *The Science of Mind*, Ernest Holmes states, "The human experience of dying is but the laying off of an old garment and the donning of a new one." As we internalize this analogy we realize there is a material body and a spiritual body. It is our belief that this spiritual body is the so-called resurrection body.

How is denial used in Science of Mind?

In Spiritual Mind Treatment, also known as Affirmative Prayer, we may use the denial of a condition as a way to lift our consciousness to see only the good (God) which we know exists beyond all appearances. In *The Science of Mind*, Ernest Holmes states, "Denial clears the way for a realization of Truth. It is a clearing of the ground, a dredging of the mental channels, preparatory to the building of a positive, constructive affirmation."

In other words, when we state a denial of a negative condition in our prayer work, this denial is always followed by a positive affirmation [See Affirmation and Treatment] because there are no voids in Mind. As we remove the belief in a negative condition through the use of denial, a positive affirmation fills that space in consciousness.

What is a demonstration?

In *The Science of Mind*, Ernest Holmes states, "We can demonstrate at the level of our ability to know." A demonstration is the result of our mental and spiritual work to know the Truth about ourselves, which creates a more rewarding life. Our demonstrations may be large or small. We should celebrate them all because they illustrate our ability to consciously know the Truth and use Principle in positive ways.

[See Principle and Truth]

Do we believe in predestination?

. . . .

Our destiny is that which we decree by what we think and embody today, producing our reality tomorrow. Our destiny is the perfect out-picturing of our individualized use of the Law of Cause and Effect.

[See Cause and Effect, Karma, and Consciousness]

Do we believe in a devil?

To believe in a devil would be to believe in duality or, in other words, to believe that there could be God as well as some opposing power. There is not a power for good and a power for evil; there is only one power and it is God. However, there are people who misuse their power. The devil is not a person, but an idea based in hellish thinking.

[See Hell]

Medically, a diagnosis is a recognition of the presence of disease, according to symptoms or conditions.

To those who practice Science of Mind, a diagnosis is nothing more than an opinion about current conditions. [See Effect] We know that while conditions may be facts, facts can also change. A diagnosis should not be ignored, because God's intelligence can be revealed in and through medical opinions; however, a diagnosis is not a verdict nor does it have to dictate the future. We know that as we do our work in consciousness, we are operating at the spiritual level. This means that we are reminding ourselves that God is First Cause to all of our experience and that in the mind of God there is no disease, nor any other discordant condition.

How can disease be healed?

In Science of Mind, disease might be defined as an impersonal thought force which operates through individuals but is not the truth about them. Because disease is an effect (or condition) it has no creative power of its own. While most people would not consciously or intentionally "think" themselves into a disease, when disease exists there is an underlying subjective belief (or cause) operating below the surface of the person's conscious awareness. This belief produces a sense of separation.

The process of healing a physical disease begins with healing the mind of all sense or belief in one's separation from Infinite Intelligence, God. As we become more aware of the presence of God at the very center of our being, inner peace will be the result [See Divine Urge]. To the degree which our creative minds become "at-ease," dis-ease in our bodies will dis-appear. God-Self awareness is the key to being at-ease.

[See Doctors & Medicine and Prayer]

What is the intention of the Divine Urge?

....

There is an inner impulse to grow that permeates the essence of all living things. In *The Science of Mind*, Ernest Holmes referred to that inner impulse to push out as the "Divine urge—the inner desire to express life...the desire to do and accomplish more...it is that eternally progressive spirit of unfoldment."

The Divine Urge moves through every living thing and its voice perpetually whispers in our inner ear, "Grow, grow, grow...I have to be more tomorrow than I was yesterday."

Because the Divine Urge is driven by the universal impulse to push out and to create "more" without judging what it is creating, it is up to us to determine what "more" shall look like. Therefore, it is wise to listen to and honor the Divine Urge by directing it in positive and productive ways. When we do so, our lives will be more fully enriched and expressed.

Do we believe in the use of doctors and medicine?

....

We believe that God is omnipresent and therefore can heal in many ways. Certainly if God is everywhere, in everyone, then the intelligence of God can and does work through the doctor's mind and hands as well as through any medication prescribed.

Of course, the ultimate goal for us as practitioners of Science of Mind is to understand that it is our thinking which creates the conditions in our bodies and the body of our affairs. It is a case of cause and effect. As we grow in our awareness of this truth, we know there will come a time when we are so fully aligned with the power and presence of God within us that there is no need for medical attention, for we are maintained in our natural state of perfection and wholeness. Perfect God, perfect human, perfect being!

What is duality and how does it affect us?

Duality is the belief in two separate and opposing powers. We heal the fear this belief fosters by experiencing God's presence within, then realizing that God is always Omnipresent.

Duality results from a fear-based belief that we are, could, or might possibly be separate from God or Good; and the imperfect appearance of "things, conditions, and individuals" in the material world seems to reinforce this belief.

We can begin by knowing it is impossible to be separated from the wholeness of God. As we live in the light of the awareness of our oneness with God, the shadows of darkness that appear to be so real begin to fade into the nothingness from which they came [See Omnipresent, Reality, and Devil].

What is embodiment, and how do we use it?

The action of embodiment is to subjectively experience a thought as a feeling of "knowing." To embody is to "give form or make part of." When we embody our thoughts and words through Spiritual Mind Treatment, we are actually allowing our thoughts to generate feelings. As our thought generates a feeling, we "give it form or make it part of" our entire being, spiritually, mentally, and physically.

Embodiment conveys to subconscious mind our acceptance of a conscious idea. We embody things constructively when we believe in what we want and want what we believe in.

Is "energy" another word for God?

Divine Energy is at the center and circumference of ALL that is. Quantum physics tells us energy is everywhere present and working even down to the subatomic level. Metaphysics tells us that energy in any form is God in action. All energy is creative. We direct energy first by understanding it and then by consciously unifying with it.

[See Divine Urge and Thought]

*What does eternity mean to us as
practitioners of Science of Mind?*

．．．．．．．．．．．．．．．．

The Eternal is the essence of God, which has no beginning
and no end. It is without time or space. There is that part
of each of us which is also eternal, because we are One in
God.

[See Death and Reincarnation]

Is evil a reality? Is there an evil power?

....

Just as there is no devil, there is no evil power. However, there are people who misuse the power they have. They use it in evil ways.

In *The Science of Mind*, Ernest Holmes states, "Evil is an experience of the soul on its journey toward the realization of Reality. Of itself, evil is neither person, place, nor thing and will disappear in exact proportion as we cease using destructive methods. As long as we make mistakes, just so long we shall be automatically punished."

[See Reality, Sin]

What constitutes faith in the teachings of Science of Mind?

In this light we can say that faith is the cornerstone upon which we build a conscious relationship with God. With enough faith in God and Life we can enter each day knowing that it is done unto us as we believe.

[See Love and Law]

What is fear and how can we deal with it?

. . . .

Metaphysically, fear is an emotional experience generated by a sense of separation from Source, God. All fear is attached to a concern of loss at some level. A full realization of God's Presence as the source and supply of whatever is needed to sustain us in wholeness, will neutralize fear. The antithesis of fear is love. Fear is the lack of the awareness of God's Presence; whereas love is the highest vibration of God's Presence.

[See Love]

Do we believe in God?

God is known by many different names such as Atman, Brahman, Allah, Baha'u'llah, The Christ, The Buddha Nature, Wakan Tanka, The Creator, The Great Maker, Jehovah, Elohim, Yahweh, The Father, The Great Spirit, The Beloved, Source, The Infinite One, Being, Presence, Self, The Whole, Divine Mind, Life, Spirit, Universal Intelligence, and even, It.

In Science of Mind God is referred to by many names as well: The First Cause, the Great I Am, the One and Only, Love, Law, Wisdom, Intelligence, Power, Substance, and Mind. God is the Truth that is real—a universal Principle that is consistent and reliable. God is Spirit or Creative Energy which is the cause of all visible things. God is the Alpha and the Omega and everything between those two points because God is all that we see and do not see.

Regardless of what name we may give God to personalize our spiritual relationship, the more we can recognize and realize the presence of God in us, and as us, the more we experience wholeness in our lives.

How do we experience God's Grace?

....

In *The Science of Mind*, Ernest Holmes states, "Grace is the givingness of Spirit to Its creation...the logical result of the correct acceptance of life and a correct relationship to the Spirit."

We do not have to pray for God's Grace because it is already given. Grace is not a gift of God's blessings to some and not others. All are equally able to live in God's Grace. The practice is for us to be mindful that Spirit is always giving Itself to us because of our oneness with God. As we live fully aware of our unity with God in the present moment we naturally enter the flow of life with grace and ease.

What is healing and where does it take place?

Because there is a direct cause and effect correlation between our minds and our bodies there must also be a direct correlation between cause and effect in the process of healing. Masters from many disciplines have echoed the same understanding regarding the relationship between our mind and our bodies, as well as the body of our affairs: "As within, so without — As above, so below — As a person thinks, so shall that person be — It is done unto you as you believe."

In *The Science of Mind*, Ernest Holmes states, "We seek to heal men's mentalities, knowing that the degree in which we are successful, we shall also be healing their bodies. Belief in duality has made man sick and the understanding of Unity will heal him."

As we work at healing our minds of the belief that we could possibly be separate from God, this healing of our belief will be reflected in the healing of conditions.

Do we believe in a Heaven?

Heaven is an inner state of happiness. We do not consider it to be a place located "up there" with pearly gates and streets paved with gold at which we shall one day arrive if we abide by a certain code of behavior. Because Heaven is a state of being and not a location, it may be experienced in the present moment. Being within, the Kingdom of Heaven can be fully experienced when we consciously bond and unify with the presence of God at the center of our very being now and every day. Every thought we have that helps us to heal any sense of separation from God can bring us closer to a Heavenly state of being.

Do we believe in a Hell?

Hell, just like Heaven, is a state of mind, all based on our awareness or lack of awareness of the presence of God within us. Hell is not a location lined with fiery pits; it is a discordant state of being where our thinking creates a sense of separation between ourselves and God. It is founded in a belief in duality, or a belief in two powers. Many people are filled with hellish thoughts and therefore experience a "living hell" every day.

[See Duality]

I Am That I Am. The "I Am" is the highest name of God.

Because God is both personal to us as well as a universal presence, the "I Am" is also both individual and universal. As we begin to walk in the "I Am" consciousness, we heal all sense of separation from God: God in me, as me, is me.

Affirming "I Am" is the most powerful statement we can make. The impartial Law of Mind operates in such a way that what we place "I Am" in front of, we tend to become.

Do we believe we are immortal beings?

....

We are more than what we see in the mirror. Knowing that God is the essence of Immortality and that we are the living embodiment of God on some level, we too must be immortal beings — perhaps not as personalities, but most certainly as spiritual beings. In *The Science of Mind* Ernest Holmes states, "If the soul can create and sustain a body here, there is no reason to deny its ability to create and sustain one hereafter." In short, the universe has made no provisions for death, only transcendence and transformation.

[See Death]

Do all people have intuition and, if so, how can it be accessed?

. . . .

In *The Science of Mind*, Ernest Holmes states, "Intuition is God in man, revealing to him the Realities of Being." Consider a radio beacon which is broadcasting its signal twenty-four hours a day. It is only when we "tune in" to the signal that we receive the information being sent. Spiritually speaking, that is how intuition works. Infinite Intelligence is making itself available to us at all times so we may be guided to our highest and best experiences in life. The same principle holds true for the animal world and the Intelligence acting in them is known as instinct. The primary difference between humans and animals is that animals have no choice but to receive and follow their natural instincts because survival depends on it; however, we do have a choice. Too often our minds and bodies are not in the same place at the same time. We can access our intuition by making time to "be still and know" and by listening to that quiet still voice that often speaks not just in our ear, but through our feeling nature as well.

[See Mindfulness and Visioning]

Was Jesus the son of God?

....

We believe that Jesus was indeed the son of God. We also believe that every other human being is the progeny of God. In *The Science of Mind*, Ernest Holmes states, "Mental Science does not deny the divinity of Jesus; but it does affirm the divinity of all people. It does not deny that Jesus was the son of God; but it affirms that all men are the sons of God."

The teachings of Jesus are paramount in Science of Mind. However, the focus is more on his understanding and use of universal principles than on his personality. Much of what Science of Mind teaches is contained in two statements credited to Jesus: "The Kingdom of Heaven is within you." (Luke 17:21) This statement affirms our oneness with God now and always. And, "It is done unto you as you believe." (Matt. 9:29) This statement affirms the power of one's thinking when aligned with one's deepest beliefs.

Jesus demonstrated perfectly how to have a relationship with the universe and with a God of love that is based on our unity with the One. In short, with deep reverence we view Jesus as the great example rather than the great exception.

How does judgment affect us?

When the teacher Jesus said, "Judge not that you shall not be judged," he was referring to the Law of Cause and Effect. Judgment is passed in our own mind based on our own experiences, and not necessarily based on the actions of the person we are judging.

Understanding that God is all there is, when we judge others (or ourselves), we create a sense of separation between ourselves and God. While it is often tempting to judge others based on their actions, perhaps Jesus understood the deeper meaning of his statement, knowing that if others are deserving of some form of punishment, the Law of Cause and Effect, which operates without judgment, always brings with it a balanced response.

There are no punishments—only consequences. When we begin to see first and foremost the Presence of God in ourselves and others we have no need or desire to judge.

[See Sin and Karma]

Do we believe in karma?

Karma is neither good nor bad, as it is not a thing in itself. It is the use we make of our mentality through the Law of Cause and Effect. Therefore, at any given moment we can begin to change our present as well as our future, because we can change our minds about the way we think and believe.

We do not recognize karma as inevitable retribution or reward, because God cannot hold judgments or grudges. As we learn from our mistakes and forgive ourselves, we let go of the past and all of its ties. This moment is our point of power, when we become the cause to a new effect or new karma.

[See Destiny]

What is the Law of Mind and how does it work?

....

The Law of Mind is the creative medium through which Spirit as Conscious Mind moves. The Law is deductive only. This means it receives the impression of thought and acts upon it much in the same way the creative medium of the earth's soil receives a seed, never rejecting it. We need to be mindful of that which we think, believe, feel, visualize, imagine, read, and talk about because it is going into the creative medium of our subconscious mind, which is our individualized use of Universal Mind. The Law of Mind is a blind force and does not judge or question the content of the thought seed. It merely says, "Yes...it is done unto you as you believe."

Whatever goes into our subconscious thought tends to return as some condition or effect. In short, the Law of Mind can be either our servant or our master, depending on how consciously we approach it and how wisely we make use of its awesome power.

[See Mind and Judgment]

Is God the essence of love?

· · · · · · · · · · · · · · · · ·

"He that loves not, knows not God; for God is Love."
(I John 4:8) In *The Science of Mind* Ernest Holmes states,
"Love is the self-givingness of the Spirit through the desire
of Life to express Itself in terms of creation.... Love is a
cosmic force whose sweep is irresistible."

Love is the highest vibration in the universe; nothing
can withstand its embrace. The opposite of love is fear. In
the light and vibration of love, the darkness of fear cannot
exist. To know God's presence is to experience unconditional love. To see the presence of God in others is to love
them. Unconditional love is always the answer.

How does the Macrocosm and the microcosm affect me?

. . . .

Spiritually speaking, the Macrocosm is the universal whole—God is all that is. The microcosm is the individuated parts of the whole, but at the same time no less than the whole in essence. Every human being represents a microcosm of the Macrocosm.

Consider the ocean as the Macrocosm and each drop of water in the ocean as the microcosm. All parts of the microcosm contain all of the essence of the whole, but they are not greater than the whole. In other words, while God is all you are, you are not all God is. The goal of Science of Mind is to support people in realizing their unique relationship, not just with God, but as mortal manifestations of God. The Macrocosm and the microcosm are one. All of the qualities of God apply to you as well. Realizing this truth will bring immense joy, health, satisfaction, abundance, tranquility, faith, power, and inner peace.

[See Universe]

What is meditation and how do we use it?

The practice of meditation has been taught by masters from every spiritual tradition for millennia because it is a foundational element in experiencing our oneness with God. Meditation is simply quieting the conscious mind to facilitate a fuller experience of God's presence. Meditation is not for the purpose of praying or receiving answers. It is after we meditate that the higher Self may be revealed in the form of guidance or desired answers [See Visioning].

There are many forms of meditation, and no particular method is better than another. All lead us to a greater experience of the One. Meditation will help instill a deep sense of inner peace and relaxation, which benefits us spiritually, mentally, and physically.

Is Science of Mind a metaphysical teaching?

· · · · · · · · · · · · · · · ·

There is nothing mysterious or supernatural about metaphysics. *Meta* means "above or beyond" and *physical* means "material, or that which is experienced by the five senses." Metaphysics includes the Science of Being, sometimes referred to as Ontology.

The study of metaphysics dates back to the time of Aristotle. It can also be thought of as the scientific study of the relational aspects of cause and effect. Metaphysics is the study of God as First Cause, Creative Intelligence or Universal Mind, which is everywhere present, [See Omnipresent] in and through all that we see, touch, smell, hear, taste...and beyond. Science of Mind is a metaphysically based teaching.

By "Mind" do we mean God's mind?

....

Yes, but we also mean our own mind, as we are all one in God. In *The Science of Mind*, Ernest Holmes states, "There is no such thing as your mind and my mind, his mind or her mind, and God's mind." In short, there is just one Mind in which all beings live, move, and express their individuality.

This Mind operates throughout our lives consciously and subconsciously. As conscious Mind it is Spirit, either in God or the individual. At the level of the subconscious Mind it is the Law in action. The subconscious Mind is always subject to conscious Mind. Spirit moves through the Law of Mind to create. That which we call "our Mind" is simply that point in God-consciousness where we are aware of Self.

[See Cause and Effect, Spirit]

What is Mindfulness and how does it affect my daily life?

Mindfulness is the practice of being consciously aware in the present moment regardless of what we are doing. Mindfulness reminds us to be one with the activity in which we are involved. When we spiritualize mindfulness it means to be present in the moment, remembering that God's presence is there as well.

Mindfulness can transform our lives in subtle as well as profound ways. When we live mindfully, connected to the presence of the Divine, everything we do becomes a sacred act. Everything we eat becomes a blessing to our bodies and every relationship we have offers us an opportunity to see the face of God.

Mindfulness encourages us to live with reverence, compassion, and generosity. In short, mindfulness can become a way of life and, in the process, our life becomes a sacred blessing to others and our world.

[See Spirituality]

What does money have to do with spirituality?

. . . .

In *The Science of Mind*, Ernest Holmes states, "Money is the symbol of God's Substance; the idea of Spiritual Supply objectified."

Quantum physics tells us that all material form is energy vibrating at a certain frequency. Money is a symbol of energy manifesting, not just as the currency itself, but also that for which the currency can be exchanged. As with all forms of energy, in order for money to serve us in life affirming ways it must remain in circulation. When we go to work we are exchanging one form of energy, our labor, for another form of energy, money. We then exchange the money for other forms of energy such as housing, food, electricity, gasoline, and so forth. The cycle of energy flowing and changing form never ceases.

When we cling to or hoard our money we impede its circulation and we become cause to the effect of "not enough" money because we have clogged the flow. It is vital to our own good to understand and practice the circulation of our money with a grateful and open heart. Remembering that God is the Source and Supply of our good is a necessary element in having a healthy relationship with money. The Law of Attraction plays a large role in fulfilling our relationship with money. Saving money is a good thing to do if it is done mindfully and without fear. Saving money can be done with wisdom backed by faith rather than fear, and the results will reflect that action. As an example consider the spare tire in the trunk of your car. Wisdom tells us to have it there, however, few people drive in fear of getting a flat tire. This is wisdom backed by faith.

It is the intention and emotional energy behind the action that triggers the "not enough" factor of the "law of attraction": If our saving is motivated by fear of not enough the universe receives the impress of that belief and impartially creates our experience to reflect it in our financial affairs. If we can apply the same "spare tire" logic regarding wisdom backed by faith in our relationship with money we shall be sending an entirely different message to a universe that always says yes.

[See Abundance, Law of Mind, Cause and Effect, Energy]

Are we part of the New Age movement?
Do we believe in the use of crystals,
channeling, psychics, hypnotism,
tarot cards or astrology?

. . . .

Science of Mind is part of the New Thought Movement, not the New Age Movement [See New Thought]. While we are in a new age of scientific discoveries and spiritual awakenings, there is nothing new about the principles we study and strive to apply in our daily lives. As New Thought, Science of Mind teaches the age-old wisdom of many of the world's great religions in a new and contemporary format. This wisdom always leads us back to the fact that our Truth and connection to God can only be found within; therefore, we feel no need to use any "tool" outside of our own consciousness to experience total wholeness, peace of mind, and a balanced life.

We do not feel the need to turn to aids or entities outside of our own innate intelligence for divine guidance or advice. To do so would be to give our power away. Science of Mind exists to help people discover their own true inner power, not to take it away from them. God is the only true power. It is First Cause and must first be found within each individual, not in the outer world. Our desire is to heal any and all notions of separation from the source of all our good—God. This is an inner experience and an age-old Truth.

Many New Thought centers and bookstores may sell "tools" that are meant to guide, teach, and help you understand your spiritual journey. Although tools are not necessary, some individuals may find comfort in using material objects that help them remember key concepts or provide inspiration.

If Science of Mind is part of the New Thought movement, what then is New Thought?

Science of Mind is one of many metaphysical teachings identified as New Thought. Since we contend there is Truth to be found in all of the world's great religions, we seek to affirm all of humankind through practicing the Presence of the One God. Therefore, with reverence and respect for all other spiritual beliefs, New Thought is a system of belief that celebrates a universal spirituality, honoring every human being as a sacred expression of the One God.

[See Religion]

What is Omnipotence?

. . . .

Omnipotent means almighty, with unlimited power. God is Omnipotence. The benefit in knowing that God is all-powerful lies in the fact that we are One with this Power. As we begin to experience the presence of God within, we know we can let this power do wonderful things through us.

This is where our power in Spiritual Mind Treatment [See Treatment] comes from. We know that we ourselves do nothing but realize the Divine Truth. It is God within that does the work.

[See Truth]

What is Omnipresence?

. . . .

The entire premise of Science of Mind rests solely on the omnipresent fact that "God Is All There Is"; God is all we see and all we don't see—all that has ever been and shall be. While we know we are not all that God is, God is all that we are.

All discord in our lives arises because at some level we have created a sense of separation from God. Our ultimate goal in Science of Mind is to heal this mistaken belief. As we practice our unity with God by experiencing God's full presence at the center and circumference of our experience, [See Absolute] a deep and fulfilling sense of Inner Peace and Wholeness will be the result. This is the Peace of God, the rock foundation of all understanding.

Each one of us is an outlet to God and an inlet to God.

— ERNEST HOLMES

What is Omniscience?

Omniscient means having complete or unlimited knowledge, awareness, or understanding; perceiving all things. The Mind of God is All-Knowing. The Truth is there has never been nor will there ever be a problem or question to which the solution or answer doesn't already exist in the Omniscient Mind of God.

Through Spiritual Mind Treatment (Affirmative Prayer), meditation, mindfulness, and visioning, we can consciously align with this Omniscient Mind of God, realizing that we already exist as One. When we do this, we begin to draw into our minds the intuition, wisdom, and courage necessary to heal and resolve our difficulties. We could begin daily to affirm and know: God in me, as me, is me, and therefore I now know what I need to know.

[See Visioning]

What is a practitioner? When and why would I use one?

....

A practitioner is a person who is trained and licensed to perform Spiritual Mind Treatment for others [see Prayer].

A practitioner does not give advice. Through treatment work, a practitioner facilitates mental and spiritual healing only, knowing all healing is done in consciousness and is reflected in the physical body and the body of one's affairs.

Because practitioners and the person for whom they are treating are both one in the mind of God, the treatment requires that practitioners know within themselves the truth *about* that person. Being one in Mind, this self-knowingness rises into the consciousness of the one being treated [See Mind, Consciousness, and Treatment].

The services of a licensed practitioner are particularly helpful when someone is emotionally entangled or too close to a problem to consciously know the Spiritual Truth about themselves.

[See Truth]

Do we pray in our teaching?

Prayer, by definition, means a "humble communication in thought or speech to God or to an object of worship expressing supplication, confession, and praise."

In Science of Mind we communicate in thought and speech with God through a process called Spiritual Mind Treatment, or affirmative prayer. We believe that God has already given us, by our divine birthright, all that we ever will need to live a complete, healthy, whole, and prosperous life; our only job is to accept it. The communication always takes place within our own consciousness and mind. Spiritual Mind Treatment is a logical process used to change our consciousness or belief system. Treatment acknowledges to Mind (or Law) that what we are treating for already exists and is ours. There is never any asking, begging, or supplication—only acceptance. The Law of Cause and Effect makes it so. Indeed, it is done unto us as we believe.

[See Treatment]

What is the Principle upon which Science of Mind is based?

....

Science of Mind has been referred to as the study of the Principle of Being. Principle is defined as: "A fundamental Truth or Law." We might say that because God Is All There Is, Principle is the Intelligence of God in action; Principle is the creative process by means of which thought becomes things.

How does Principle operate? By means of each of us, the Intelligence of God, as conscious mind, moves through a field of subconscious mind (or creative medium), creating a result (or effect). Knowing that we all exist in the one Mind of God, we each individualize this Principle every time we think and feel. As we understand the purpose and function Principle, we can then choose to enable positive changes in our lives. Principle is *never* bound by precedent.

[See Law]

Does God punish us when we "break the rules"?

First and foremost, God places no rules or expectations on us. We have absolute dominion over our own lives and the ability to choose our own course of action. In other words, we have been given free will to create our own experience. If we choose to think or act in a way that is not life affirming for the good of all concerned, we will experience negative consequences as a result of the Universal Law of Cause and Effect. Since God does not judge, there is no such thing as punishment; there are only consequences.

[See Cause & Effect, Karma, and Sin]

What is Reality?

....

We live in a world that believes if something looks, feels, or smells like reality, it must be real. In essence, though, it is actually our unreality. The ultimate "Reality" is the absolute truth, which behind all form is the formless energy, essence, and intelligence of God.

Quantum physics tells us that everything in the material world is energy vibrating at a specific frequency and is held in place by that vibration. Therefore, the apparent reality (that which we see, touch, and smell) is just that—it appears to be something, and it is always subject to change as the vibration changes.

Ultimate Reality, however, is the unformed pure Essence of the Divine. It is changeless perfection; therefore, the Real Self is perfection, for God could not know anything unlike Itself. The spirit of God within us and all around us is the only true reality. As we begin to get in touch daily with this perfect principle, we can then demonstrate it in our daily lives. Perfect God, Perfect Human, Perfect Being—this is the Absolute Truth.

[See Absolute and Relative]

What is realization?

A realization is an impression of Reality on the mind. A realization may be experienced as a divine "Ah-ha!" It's an awareness of God's presence, infused within us and around us in whatever we are saying or doing. As we mindfully practice the awareness of God's presence as our Reality it will then become more fully realized and thus manifested in our daily lives.

[See Reality]

Do we believe in reincarnation?

In *The Science of Mind*, Dr. Ernest Holmes states, "The spiral of life is upward. Evolution carries us forward, not backward. Eternal and progressive expansion is law and there are no breaks in continuity....I can believe in planes beyond this one without number, in eternal progress. I cannot believe that nature is limited to one sphere of action."

Life is an eternal flow, and we are streams of consciousness within this flow, forever unfolding [See Eternal and Destiny]. The question of reincarnation is meaningless when we accept the fact that at some level we have always been and shall always be. Living in the present moment is what matters now.

What do we mean by the word Relative?

The relative is that which depends on something else for its existence. In Science of Mind, the relative is anything we can relate with or experience with the five senses of sight, hearing, touch, taste, and smell. While the relative world may appear as conditions separate from the All, it is not. God is all there is. [See Absolute, Reality, and Universe]

In the beginning, there was only God, with the desire to be more fully expressed. To do this, God created form which surrounds the core essence of Being, just as clothing on the body. Hence, the relative. The relative is really another term for the Body of God. God is Absolute and Relative!

Is Science of Mind considered a religion or philosophy?

It has been said that Science of Mind is a correlation of laws of science, opinions of philosophy, and revelations of religion applied to the needs and aspirations of humankind. Perhaps Science of Mind is both a religion and a philosophy...and more.

Any religion is simply the framework that supports a common spiritual notion. The word "religion" comes from the Greek/Latin word *religare*, which means "to bind together." All religions purport to assist their followers in realizing their unity with one another and God. This is what Science of Mind teaches.

It seems, however, that many of the world's religions have done just the opposite, dividing the world and separating people not only from one another but also from God. Throughout history more wars have been fought in the name of God than for any other reason because one religion deemed itself to be the "right" one.

We believe there are many paths to the one God and we honor each individual's chosen path. Our founder, Ernest Holmes, was an avid student of the world's great religions and was influenced by the common thread he found running through many of them. When synthesized by his own consciousness, this common thread became the foundational principles of Science of Mind.

[See Science of Mind]

What is Religious Science?

In 1926 Ernest Holmes wrote *The Science of Mind*, a book which became the basis for a metaphysical teaching that has since spread around the world. In 1927 he established the Institute of Religious Science and Philosophy in Los Angeles to expand upon the teaching and the principles he wrote about in the book. Eventually some of the graduates from the Institute began to found churches based on the teaching. While it was not his desire to create churches or a "religion" he ultimately agreed and the denomination became known as Religious Science.

Eventually several branches of the Religious Science denomination developed. One was the United Church of Religious Science and the other, Religious Science International. Ultimately, in 2008, the two organizations decided to become one—based in Golden Colorado—branding themselves as Centers for Spiritual Living (CSL). The organization's mission is to provide spiritual tools for personal and global transformation. Their purpose is to awaken humanity to its spiritual magnificence, and their vision is a world that works for everyone.

RESURRECTION

How does the principle of resurrection apply to me personally?

On one level, resurrection can be looked at as a metaphor illustrating the fact that there is no such thing as death, only a sacred continuum of life eternal which is never limited to one dimension or form. This is the message seen in the resurrection of Jesus. [See Death and Immortality]

On yet another level, we can see that God's presence is a sustaining life Principle that is ever-present within us, renewing our vitality and life force in our day-to-day lives. When we "remember to remember" this truth, we are literally resurrected each day to a new life in our unity with God. In challenging times this can be important to keep in mind. As Paul reminds us in Romans 12:2 — "Be transformed by the renewing of your mind."

What is Right Action and how does it work?

. . . .

In *The Science of Mind*, Ernest Holmes states, "When we treat for right action we should start with the supposition that right action already is."

In metaphysics, right action is not referring to a code of behavior or right conduct such as what might be found in the Buddha's Eight-Fold Path. Right action is the natural unfoldment of the universe as it evolves towards the highest and ultimate good. When we align with the principle of right action we find inner peace from knowing that there is an Infinite Intelligence at work in the universe that knows what it is doing.

We do not pray for right action to happen because it already is happening. Instead, we can pray to know and accept that right action is always unfolding, even when circumstances may appear otherwise.

Is Jesus our savior?

Jesus was a way-shower and master teacher who knew the divine Truth about himself and all others. We do not believe he died on a cross to save us from sin. [See Sin]

We look to the teacher Jesus as the great example rather than the great exception. In Science of Mind we make no attempt to deny Jesus of his greatness or refute his teachings. If anything, Science of Mind is partially based on his teachings. "The works that I do shall you do also; and greater works than these you shall do." Therein lies the divine potential for all humankind.

What is the Science of Mind?

. . . .

The Science of Mind is the title of the book written by Dr. Ernest Holmes in 1926 and revised by him in 1938. It became the text and basis for the teaching of Science of Mind as a science, philosophy, and religion for many thousands of people worldwide. After the publication of *The Science of Mind* Ernest Holmes wrote many other books currently being used by eager students of Science of Mind worldwide.

As a science, Science of Mind is based on specific universal principles that many of the world's leading scientists are now proving. As a philosophy, Science of Mind is a simple, practical, and down-to-earth way of understanding the full nature of the Universe and our relationship to it. As a religion, Science of Mind represents a synthesis of many of the world's greatest spiritual teachings, explained in a logical and applicable manner that brings hundreds of thousands of people together weekly for Sunday celebration services and classes.

For the dedicated student, Science of Mind is not just a teaching but a way of life.

Do we believe that people are sinners?

. . . .

The word *sin* comes from an ancient Greek term. When an archer missed the target with his arrow, he sinned. Sin means to miss the mark or to make a mistake.

In The Science of Mind, Ernest Holmes states, "There is no sin but a mistake, and no punishment but a consequence." The Law of Cause and Effect always brings with it the consequences of the action or mistake. Holmes goes on to say, "God does not punish sin. As we correct our mistakes, we forgive our own sins."

It is impossible to believe that God (who is present in all forms of life) would deem humans less than perfect because God is a God of love, not anger, judgment, or punishment. God does, however, allow us to answer for our own mistakes (sins) to the immutable Law of Cause and Effect. There is no good or bad—there are only consequences.

As we grow, deepening our understanding of the relationship between our thinking, the choices we make, and how the Law of Cause and Effect operates, we shall indeed learn to "sin" no more.

[See Karma, and Cause & Effect]

Do we believe that we have a soul?

We believe there is only one Soul and it is the Soul of the Universe. Our individual soul is simply that point within us where the Universe (or God) is personalized.

We believe that the soul is our creative medium and is therefore subject to our conscious thought. Soul receives the imprint of our deepest beliefs and acts to bring them into manifest form in our experience. In other words, the soul is that perfect part of our being which accepts us and our actions, never judging us as right or wrong, always ready to assist us in achieving whatever we choose to do when we believe we can do it. The soul has been referred to as the "mirror of mind," because it reflects the forms of thought which are given it. The most important thing to remember is that it is we who choose the thoughts the Soul reflects.

[See Law]

Does each person have a spirit?

More than that, every person actually is spirit. We believe that since the Spirit of God desired to be more fully expressed, the form was created to transport and release the expression.

That form comes in many different shapes. Among the highest forms of God's expression is the human form— You. We are each the Spirit of God individualized. Rather than trying as human beings to have a "spiritual experience," we should imagine life from the viewpoint that we are primarily spiritual beings having a human experience. You are not just a body of flesh and bones. There is a self-confident, free-choosing, empowered spirit at the center of your being.

As we become more aware of the presence of the spirit that we really are, we automatically begin to live in the awareness that God and each individual are truly one. Spirit is where the creative process originates: Spirit thinks consciously, sending this thought through the creative and subjective mind and becomes objectified in our outer world of effect. Spirit is the cause; the result of the thought is the effect.

[See Law of Mind]

How does Spirituality apply to me personally?

• • • • • • • • • • • • • • • • • •

Because we know God is all there is, we know we live in a spiritual universe. The reality is we could not be any more "spiritual" than we already are regardless of how hard we might try. We are already 100% spirit. Spirituality is merely the conscious practice of the awareness of God's presence in the present moment.

This is why our spiritual practices are so important—they serve as our daily reminder to "remember to remember" that we are one with the Divine, now and always.

[See Mindfulness, Meditation, Treatment, and Visioning]

• •

What is Thought?

In Science of Mind we know that our thoughts are energy being directed in a specific way. The creative process begins with a belief which then brings forth a specific thought— it is a movement of consciousness [See Consciousness].

Our thought originates as cause in our conscious mind, which then moves through our subconscious mind as Law. In other words, our thoughts work through Law, but that Law is consciously set in motion. (This is how thoughts become things.)

To consciously apply the Law [See Law and Embody] the initial step requires the realization that we are responsible for the thoughts we think and control. Change your thining, change your life.

What is a Treatment and how does it affect me?

. . . .

In Science of Mind, a "Treatment" (also known as a Spiritual Mind Treatment) is simply an affirmative prayer stated in a systematic manner (or formula). It usually has five steps that guide you or the person performing the treatment through a logical flow of statements that reinforce our unity with God [See Prayer]. An example of a simplified Treatment might be:

1. I know God is All there is.
2. I know I am one with God, in Spirit, Mind, and Body.

3. I know that the good I seek already exists in the mind of God.

4. Knowing I am one with God and that the gift has already been made, I claim and accept my good, giving great thanks for it.

5. I now release this prayer unto the Universe, knowing it is done, as I believe. I let go and let God. And so it is. Amen.

A Spiritual Mind Treatment does not cause change to any physical conditions initially. It does however change the consciousness of the one being treated. Because we all exist in the one mind of God, what is known as the truth in the consciousness of the one doing the treatment, elevates an awareness in the experience of the one being treated.

[See Practitioner]

What is Truth?

In *The Science of Mind*, Ernest Holmes states, "Truth...is the Reason, Cause and Power in and through everything. It is Birthless, Deathless, Changeless, Complete, Perfect, Whole, Self-Existent, Causeless, Almighty, God, Spirit, Law, Mind, Intelligence, and anything and everything that implies Reality."

When the teacher Jesus said, "Know the truth and the truth shall set you free," he meant the truth about yourself. From that truth, you will be free and able to direct your own life in wonderful, creative, meaningful ways, simply by understanding that your every thought is a creative expression of the truth. Remember, God is all that is. "God in you, as you, *is* you." Know this truth and you are free to express your true Self!

What is the Universe?

. . . .

The Universe is the body of God. The Universe is that which was created in order to more fully express the best and highest good. [See Relative]

Scientists tell us the Universe is continually expanding. This is the creative divine urge of God to grow. This same creative divine urge permeates every cell in our bodies. It is that urge which causes us to grow and be more than we were yesterday. Our bodies are simply mini-universes, the microcosm within the Macrocosm.

[See Macrocosm & Microcosm]

What is Visioning and how is it different than visualization?

. . . .

The Life Visioning Process™ originated by Michael Bernard Beckwith is a spiritual practice designed to activate one's inherent intuitive ability. It is based on the principle that Divine Intelligence is everywhere present [See Omnipresence] and seeks to express itself by means of us. Visioning may be applied to all aspects of life including creative ventures, simple problem solving, or uncovering the next step in one's evolution. It is a process that can be done in groups of people seeking to find an answer of common interest, or the process can be done by an individual.

The basic steps include centering within until reaching an interior stillness, followed by inquiry such as: "What is seeking to emerge through me?"; "What must I become to manifest this vision?"; "What must I release to manifest this vision?"; "What talents, gifts, and capacities do I already have that can serve this vision?" After asking each question, the individual(s) remains in meditative silence to receive guidance from the Higher Self. A Visioning session closes with gratitude for what has been revealed.

An important key is to understand that Visioning employs one's intuition, while visualization employs the imagination. By first Visioning and intuitively catching a vision, it is then possible to set the intention and goals for its fulfillment in one's life structures.

[See Intuition]

In what context do we use the term, the Word?

....

In *The Science of Mind*, Ernest Holmes states, "The Word means, of course, the ability of Spirit to declare an expression into manifestation, into form. The word of God means the Self Contemplation of the Spirit."

This means that both the physical elements of the Universe which we see, as well as the invisible essence of the Universe we don't see, constitute the Self-Contemplation of God. The "I Am that I Am." In the beginning was the Word.

This is meaningful to us because as incarnations of the One Spirit of God, each time we think or contemplate, we are really speaking the "Word" into creative mind and through the law of cause and effect, our "Word" becomes manifest. At the beginning of any creative process is the Word—the Infinite Intelligence of God-First Cause, moving from thought to thing. That which we place the words "I Am" in front of, we become. This is the creative power of the Word.

SUMMARY

The teaching of Science of Mind has one primary purpose: To assist individuals who desire, and are willing do the necessary work, to heal their life of any and all discord, fear, superstition, guilt, and sense of lack. Wholeness is a Reality and it can be found at the very center of who and what we are now. In the process of creating a better life for ourselves we add something of great meaning and worth to the world.

The intention of Science of Mind is not to instruct willing individuals in what to think but rather in how to think. We can best learn how to think by first understanding that we live in a Spiritual Universe that operates on purpose, by responding to our thoughts, feelings, and deepest beliefs.

It is you and you alone who ultimately creates your experience. While this Truth may at times be challenging to accept, it is also the Truth which makes you free.

As we learn to take responsibility for our thinking, we shall see our lives transformed in incredible and wonderful ways. We can begin to live, move, and express our true nature in a greater awareness that God is All that is. As we honor God's Presence in all people and places (including ourselves, wherever we may be) the Divine Principle of Life automatically honors us.

In the conclusion of the Science of Mind textbook, Dr. Ernest Holmes summarized this all very well when he wrote, "The practice of Truth is personal to each, and in the long run no one can live our life for us. To each is given what he needs and the gifts of heaven come alike to all. How we shall use these gifts is all that matters!"

In other words, there is a Power for good in the Universe, greater than you and you can use it now. This is God's gift to you--and what you decide to do with it is your gift to God!

DECLARATIONS
AND PRINCIPLES

WE BELIEVE in God, the Living Spirit Almighty, one, indestructible, absolute and self-existent Cause. This One manifests Itself in and through all creation, but is not absorbed by Its creation. The manifest universe is the body of God. It is the logical and necessary outcome of the infinite self-knowingness of God.

WE BELIEVE in the individualization of the Spirit in Us, and that all people are individualizations of the One Spirit.

WE BELIEVE in the eternality, the immortality, and the continuity of the individual soul, forever and ever expanding.

WE BELIEVE that Heaven is within us and that we experience to the degree that we become conscious of It.

WE BELIEVE the ultimate goal of life to be a complete freedom from all discord of every nature, and that this goal is sure to be attained by all.

WE BELIEVE in the unity of all life, and that the highest God and the innermost God is one God. We believe that God is personal to all who feel this Indwelling Presence.

WE BELIEVE in the direct revelation of Truth through the intuitive and spiritual nature, and that anyone may become a revealer of Truth who lives in close contact with the Indwelling God.

WE BELIEVE that the Universal Spirit, which is God, operates through a Universal Mind, which is the Law of God, and that we are surrounded by this Creative Mind which receives the direct impress of our thought and acts upon it.

WE BELIEVE in the healing of the sick through the power of this Mind.

WE BELIEVE in the control of conditions through the power of this Mind.

WE BELIEVE in the eternal Goodness, the eternal Lovingkindness, and the eternal Givingness of Life to all.

WE BELIEVE in our own soul, our own spirit, and our own destiny, for we understand that the life all is God.

—Ernest Holmes

For more information, please visit your local Center for Spiritual Living, Religious Science, or Science of Mind church, or contact one of the following organizations:

Centers for Spiritual Living
573 Park Point Dr.
Golden, Co 80401
(720) 496-1370
www.csl.org

Affiliated New Thought Network
7918 El Cajon Blvd., Suite N332
La Mesa, CA 91942
(831) 372-1159
www.newthought.org

ABOUT THE AUTHOR

Having been a motivational force in New Thought for over thirty-five years, Dennis Merritt Jones, D.D. has often been referred to as "a teacher's teacher." Throughout his lifetime, Dennis has been on a quest to inspire and lift people to a higher expression of life. His personal vision is to guide people to their purpose, knowing that when a person fully awakens to who they are and why they are on the planet, they begin to naturally share their gift with humankind and, in the process, create an enriching life for themselves and the world around them.

In addition to *How to Speak Science of Mind*, Dennis is also the author of a number of award winning books:

The Art of Abundance ~ Ten Rules for a Prosperous Life

The Art of Uncertainty ~ How to Live In the Mystery of Life and Love It.

The Art of Being ~ 101 Ways to Practice Purpose In Your Life

Your (Re)Defining Moments ~ Becoming Who You Were Born to Be

Encouraging Words ~ Articles & Essays That Prove Who You Are Matters

(All of Dennis' books can be ordered through DeVorss Publications.)

Dennis believes we each have the capacity and, ultimately, the responsibility to contribute something positive to this world, leaving it a better place than it was when we arrived. His teachings promote a contemporary, life-affirming, spiritually logical and positive outlook on life, which are reflected in his writings. Dennis was the founder and spiritual director of the International Center for Spiritual Living in Simi Valley, CA. He retired from the pulpit in 2008 after twenty-three years to take his message to the world by means of his books, spiritual mentoring, keynote speaking and seminars. For more information please visit his website. www.DennisMerrittJones.com